Penguin Books

D1542346

The Blitz: The Photography of George Rodger

As a photographer for *Life* magazine, George Rodger covered many aspects of the Second World War, including the London Blitz in 1940 as it affected the lives of ordinary English people. After the London Blitz, he went from West Africa through Eritrea and Ethiopia to Iran, then to the north-west frontier of India with the British Army, before coming back to Tobruk and the Western Desert. He was in the Burma Campaign with the Chinese, landed in North Africa with the American forces and continued with them for the landings in Sicily and at Salerno. He went through the Italian Campaign with British troops and Gurkhas, landed in Normandy on D-Day with the British Army, crossed the Rhine with Churchill and Montgomery in 1945 and covered the German surrender at Luneberg. His coverage of war ended with the horrifying experience of entering Belsen.

He left *Life* magazine in 1947 and joined Robert Capa, Henri Cartier-Bresson and David Seymour in founding the most famous of all picture agencies, Magnum Photos. He went to Africa and travelled and lived among the Masai of Kenya and the Nuba of the Upper Nile, some of whom had never seen a white man before. He brought back a record of their everyday life such as no other photographer has ever made.

THE BLITZ

The Photography of George Rodger

with an Introduction by Tom Hopkinson

Penguin Books

I should like to thank Charles Hennessy, Jeffrey Simmons, Tony Lacey, Fiona Carpenter, Kate Judd, Charles Drazin, Tessa Strickland and my wife Jinx for their enthusiasm and help in compiling this book.

Note: The majority of these photographs were taken in London or, as indicated, in Dover.
Photographs that were taken in Coventry appear on the following pages: 35–6, 59–67, 73, 132–3, 138–9.

PENGUIN BOOKS

Published by the Penguin Group
27 Wrights Lane, London W8 5TZ, England
Viking Penguin, a division of Penguin Books USA Inc.
375 Hudson Street, New York, New York 10014, USA
Penguin Books Australia Ltd, Ringwood, Victoria, Australia
Penguin Books Canada Ltd, 2801 John Street, Markham, Ontario, Canada L3R 1B4
Penguin Books (NZ) Ltd, 182–190 Wairau Road, Auckland 10, New Zealand

Penguin Books Ltd, Registered Offices: Harmondsworth, Middlesex, England

First published 1990

1 3 5 7 9 10 8 6 4 2

Copyright © George Rodger, 1990
Introduction copyright © Tom Hopkinson, 1990
All rights reserved
The moral right of the author has been asserted

Filmset in 9/14pt Linotron Franklin Gothic
Printed and bound in Great Britain by Butler & Tanner Ltd, Frome and London

Contents

Introduction by *Tom Hopkinson*

To everyone who lived –
and died – in the Blitz

At first glance, George Rodger's photographs of the London Blitz appear surprisingly quiet, almost indeed peaceful. Here are no warehouses blasted into streets; no heroic

INTRODUCTION

firemen stagger through blazing infernos; no piles of corpses wait to be identified. What George Rodger gives us is the ordinary man or woman in extraordinary situations; the normalities and decencies of everyday life, surviving amid the horrors of a war waged with modern weapons of destruction against a civilian population.

An elderly citizen in suit and Homburg hat sweeps up the shattered windows of the shop that provides his living – or did so until last night.

Out in the suburbs a husband, who looks like an office-worker, carries the furniture out of a house whose roof has been blown off and its windows sucked out by blast, and carefully stacks whatever is still usable on what used to be the lawn.

In front of an impromptu Information Centre a dozen or so people have collected. Quietly, without any pushing or shoving, they peer over one another's shoulders to examine typed lists of names. Chalked on the wall above is the instruction:

ENQUIRIES RE CASUALTIES ON TOP FLOOR
RE DEATHS ON FIRST FLOOR

One of the few soldiers to be seen on this domestic battle-front stands in Trafalgar Square. A pigeon sits on his head, and there

are two more which he is feeding on his arm. Elsewhere, following an arduous night, two Civil Defence workers – in collars and ties, steel helmets and carrying gas-masks – engage in the familiar routine of the morning cuppa.

The world of the Blitz was a world in which the everyday and the unthinkable existed side by side, with the two continually changing places. The courage of so-called 'ordinary' people was shown by the way they passed from one to the other without breaking down or cracking up. To those living through the Blitz, it often seemed that life was divided by the clock: factory, office or domestic routine by day; hell and devastation let loose when darkness fell. Chiefly it is the near-normality of daytime – the efforts to tidy the place up and get on with the routine, rather than the night-time heroics – that forms the background to George Rodger's pictures.

Let no one suppose, however, that because his photographs concentrate mainly on the normalities, they were therefore easy to take; or that, being free from artifice or photographic tricks – appearing to have happened, not to have been designed – anyone with a camera might have taken them. The particular skill of George Rodger is to conceal his skill. The photographer never comes between subject and viewer; it is, in a sense, his absence which allows the scene to happen.

Direct, simply but strongly composed, taken at a sufficient distance to show people in their everyday setting, calmly inhabiting the world with which they are familiar, these pictures of the Blitz convey a message which is unmistakable but never stressed: 'This is how it was. This is how life went on.' There is an absence of drama which is totally convincing.

Few photographers have travelled so far, so continuously and so dangerously as George Rodger; few have visited so many countries, made contact with so many races and peoples. After the London Blitz, he went for *Life* magazine from West Africa through Eritrea and Ethiopia to Iran. Then to the north-west frontier of India with the British Army, before coming back to Tobruk and the Western Desert. He was in the Burma Campaign with the Chinese; landed in North Africa with the American forces; continued with them for the landings in Sicily and at Salerno. He went through the Italian Campaign with British troops and Gurkhas, landed in Normandy on D-Day with the British Army, crossed the Rhine with Churchill and Montgomery in 1945, and covered the German surrender at Luneberg.

Rodger's war ended with the horrifying experience of entering Belsen, and he determined to cover no more wars. Throughout it all his fixed resolve was 'to show things as they are'. He would employ no tricks or subterfuge, take part in no dramatizations or 'reconstructions'.

Having parted with *Life* magazine in 1947, George Rodger joined Robert Capa, Henri Cartier-Bresson and David Seymour in founding the most famous of all picture agencies, Magnum Photos. When each of its members chose a territory in which to operate, George Rodger chose Africa. Travelling and living among so-called 'primitive' peoples – such as the Masai of Kenya and the Nuba of the Upper Nile, some of whom had never seen a white man previously – he brought back a record of their everyday life, secret ceremonies and rituals such as no other photographer has ever made. Asked what had made this possible, his answer was typical and revealing.

I could never have got my Masai pictures, if handling my camera hadn't become second nature to me, a matter of reflexes as instinctive as opening one's mouth to bite an apple. But in such situations the technical side is the least part of it; what's vital is the contact you make with the people you're among. Basically, this is a matter of the respect and liking you feel for them, and which somehow they understand and feel towards you in return.

Ten years ago, a writer in a magazine which no longer exists, *Art and Artists*, said of George Rodger's African pictures: 'What he does is to photograph in a way that brings out the inherent nobility of his subjects.' Precisely the same can be said of his photographs of Londoners during the Blitz. The writer defines this as 'a kind of genius ... it evinces a quality that Victorian writers might have called spiritual greatness.' True; but why in 1990 need we shelter behind unnamed Victorian writers? George Rodger's photographs – taken in the Blitz, in Africa, and over half the world – are his explicit statement of the brotherhood of man and the essential value of every human being. And this is surely the only basis on which spiritual greatness can exist.

Tom Hopkinson

Although war with Germany was not declared until 3 September 1939, we in Britain had been noticing much writing on the wall that made us apprehensive for the future.

What were we to expect?

Gas attack?

Parachute landings?

It was the great uncertainty that most

1 MAKING READY

In 1938 Austria was annexed by Germany and Chamberlain reached his far from reassuring Munich Agreement.

In the spring of 1939, Herr Adolph Hitler annexed Bohemia and Moravia, and denounced the Anglo-German Naval Agreement. In the summer he signed a pact with Soviet Russia and invaded Poland.

There was no doubt in our minds that war would come – April 1939 saw the introduction of conscription and the mobilization of the British fleet. But it looked at first as though Herr Hitler would catch us with our pants down. In anticipation of the kind of catastrophe that was overtaking Poland, over a million people were evacuated to places of greater safety during the week that led up to the declaration of war.

Compulsory military service was made law on 2 September and, on the next day, war was declared with Germany.

Hitler ranted and raved in Munich.

'Deutschland über alles!'

Immediately after the radio announcement that we were at war, the air-raid siren wailed above us. We were not to know it was triggered off by Lord Lloyd returning unexpectedly from Cairo and we waited, somewhat tense I must admit, for whatever horrors Hitler had in store for us.

Nerves twanged like harp-strings.

wracked our nerves.

Actually nothing happened in London for a whole year to come and, by that time, we had settled down.

But, in the meantime, with a grim determination we set about our preparations for the conflict.

Compulsory black-out was enforced immediately. All windows had to be screened by light-proof black curtains. Headlamps were masked and ladies of easy virtue around Piccadilly and Marble Arch held lighted candles in cupped hands. In anticipation of parachute landings, signposts all over Britain had been removed by the spring of 1940 and it was a risky business to stop in the countryside and ask the locals for directions. They were trigger-happy with their pitchforks.

As early as April 1939, in anticipation of a manpower shortage once the war began, Government training centres, for both men and women, had been opened in many parts of the country. These were intended to help engineering and machine shops make the planes and tanks and guns that we were so lamentably short of, and to supplement the supply of raw materials. Ornamental iron railings were melted down for guns, and the recycling of paper and glass was widespread.

London was an ant's nest of activity – air-raid shelters were built in the streets; Anderson shelters (named after the Home Secretary, Sir John Anderson) erected in suburban gardens; Local Defence Volunteers (later to be called the Home Guard) were busy practising defence tactics. Women volunteers organized distribution centres for food and clothing. Everyone was madly buying Defence Bonds or 3 $1/_2$% National Savings Certificates.

A vulnerable point in London's defences was the Thames estuary. Amateur yachtsmen, with some help from the Navy, formed the River Patrol, operating day and night. Around London, barrage balloons, each anchored to a lorry and manned by a crew of eight men, were flown as defence against low-flying aircraft.

The immediate cutting down of all commodities to bare essentials in both material and quality gave rise to the term 'utility' fashion. Girls on ARP (Air Raid Patrol) adopted boiler suits, or woollen cloaks with hoods. Gloves with white palms (sometimes luminous) were introduced to show up in the dark.

After sundown no light was permitted. Dense light-proof black cloth covered all windows. Car headlights (for those who still ran cars) had to be heavily masked. Other black-out measures included painting white strips on to street bollards and on to the sides of cars. Policemen on night patrol wore white sleeve-cuffs.

We were as prepared as we could be under the circumstances and the total involvement of everyone boosted morale, as did the distribution of gas-masks to every man, woman and child in the country.

A stalwart customer at The Cause Has Altered public house, Dover.

11

A battery of press men on Shakespeare Cliff, Dover, wait to photograph the expected invasion.

Eric Sevareid reporting live to the USA on a German raid off the south coast.

Barrage balloons being anchored on the Dover seafront opposite the Grand Hotel.

Barrage-balloon crews in
training at RAF Cardington.

The civilian 'River Patrol'...

... and two of its organizers.

A 'Home Guard' of employees in a Whitehall government ministry.

Private cars display notices offering free lifts to pedestrians unlucky enough to be caught on the streets during an air raid.

Black-out regulations (left and pp. 21–5). All headlamps on vehicles are shielded so as to cast only a dim beam downwards.

**Policemen are issued with
white sleeve-cuffs.**

Street lamps are brightly painted with white stripes.

Gloves are lined with white
kid to show up in the dark.   23

Fashions had to become both economical ...

... and functional.

The threat of invasion and nightly bombing creates a common denominator in which all men are equal – all women too. Bombs are not selective and women in the Blitz were as

2 WOMEN AT WORK

vulnerable as men. They, therefore, shared the work with the menfolk as they shared the risks and, as more men were called up for the forces, so more women took their places at home. They worked in the factories and in the fields. They manned the searchlights that ringed London and the anti-aircraft-gun placements on the coast. They trained as engineers – civil and even marine. They became air-raid wardens, ARP (Air Raid Patrol) shelter supervisors, secretaries in the Ministries, nurses, emergency first-aiders. They manned post offices and telephone exchanges and worked on the London Underground. They became canteen workers, drivers, mechanics, couriers, and handled any jobs that needed doing, however menial.

Working conditions were spartan and the lack of heating started a fad for side-coiled hair-styles to keep the ears warm. The working week was usually forty-eight hours – but could be longer. A non-stop, round-the-clock BBC broadcast, *Music While You Work*, which included such songs as 'Dance, Dance, Dance Little Lady', 'Goodnight Sweetheart' and 'Smoke Gets In Your Eyes', helped to make the time pass quickly.

Those who had never had to work before did not find it easy to master metalwork ...

... but they persevered.

Women being instructed in the skills of technical drawing.

**The underground telephone
exchange in Whitehall.**

Eager pupils studying blueprints.

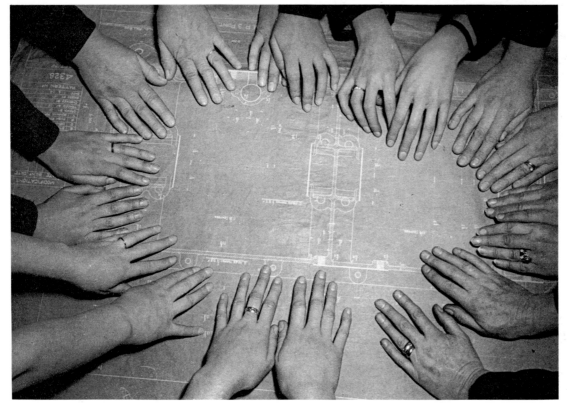

Factory hands – no more manicures or painted nails.

An art student decorates
hoardings on the shattered
shop fronts of Oxford Street.

Civilian women learn to
operate the machinery left
idle by men departing for
military service.

A machine shop floor staffed
entirely by women.

33

The German invasion of Britain, code-named 'Sea Lion', was scheduled for 5 September 1940. Hitler thundered 'Total Annihilation' as he had done over Poland and Holland. He

docks. Daylight raids began. Goering sought a knock-out blow.

A massive 400-bomber blitz on the docks set the East End of London alight. The planes

3 BLITZ AND RESCUE

expected his blitzkrieg to overwhelm Britain in a matter of days. But Grand Admiral Raeder, who was in charge of the invasion fleet, realized that it was totally inadequate, and he told the Führer to delay the invasion until the spring of 1941.

The porcine commander of the Luftwaffe, Hermann Goering, Reichsmarschall no less, had done his homework and was more realistic than his Führer. He realized that no invasion could succeed until the RAF was muzzled.

He code-named his aerial blitzkrieg 'Eagle' and proceeded to harass the airfields of Fighter Command in Kent and Sussex. The small force of RAF fighter planes was vastly outnumbered and, by 15 September, wave after wave of bombers and strafing dive-bombers had temporarily inactivated five of the seven airfields. These were Manston, Lympne, Detling, Hawkinge and West Malling. Biggin Hill remained operational but the surviving pilots were close to the end of their tether.

Meanwhile, the first bomb fell on London during the night of 24–5 August 1940. This was not in fact a deliberate attempt to attack the capital – the bombs were said to have been jettisoned by a pilot returning from an abortive raid on an airfield. Churchill retaliated by ordering massive attacks on Berlin. An infuriated Hitler now called off Goering's Eagle operation and targeted our urban factories and

came in droves, hundreds at a time, with a fluctuating drone of engines so loud it eclipsed all other sound and seemed to possess one's very being and leave the mind all windmills. Then, after dark, the night bombers moved in, guided to their target by incendiary fires on either side of the river. Stirring times. Many civilians died in the raids but England was saved and the downfall of the Reich began.

On that Saturday night of 7 September, 430 East-Enders lost their lives. On Sunday 412 were killed and on the Monday the toll was 370. But then, at last, our anti-aircraft guns went into action and their loud bark was comforting. The raids continued for seventy-six consecutive nights (bar one night when there was a dense fog). The banshee wail of the warning siren, followed by the distant rumble of the bombers growing ever louder, became an accepted part of our lives, as did the welcome music of the guns. I could not sleep of a night until the guns opened up. They were particularly active on bright nights when raids were heaviest. I called them my Moonlight Sonata.

Once the Blitz was really under way, both private and public life was severely disrupted. None of us knew when or where the next bombs would fall, but everywhere was a potential target. At the end of the working day, business men donned steel helmets to work as air-raid wardens or members of volunteer rescue

10

Coventry, 15 November 1940.
Coventry Cathedral was still
intact after this raid.

An air-raid warden finds a telephone that's still working.

services. With enemy planes often overhead and bombs falling, railway station-masters endeavoured to dispel gloom by playing cheerful music through loudspeakers. In the early morning, bus routes had to be constantly changed to avoid streets blocked by rubble from the night's raids.

Voluntary rescue squads worked throughout the night during the raids. The Heavy Rescue Squad, made up for the most part of men who had previously worked for demolition and construction companies, was in particular demand. When the raiders departed and the guns were silent, we could hear pitiful cries from under tons of rubble. For some there was help; for others, none. There is an acrid smell to high explosives and a sweet smell to death. Neither is pleasant. In the Blitz, it hung in the air chokingly as it mingled with the dust and black smoke of burning buildings.

Some people were badly shell-shocked by the attacks, but a remarkable number rallied their spirits. After heavy raids, I would often see housewives and children in bomb-blasted homes joking lightly with passers-by, and shopkeepers out in the early morning resolutely tidying up shattered glass and rubble.

Thursday 14 November was the night of the 'Baedecker' raid, when German planes attacked five of England's cathedral cities, which were virtually undefended. The hardest-hit was Coventry – a prime target throughout the Blitz, since many of the local car firms had changed over to aircraft manufacture and the production of armaments. As the charred ruins continued to smoulder after the night-long raid, I watched the city slowly come to life again. Many bombed-out residents were evacuated; food supplies were rapidly organized for those who remained. Life had to go on – but postmen on their rounds found many addresses missing.

Meanwhile, the pilots of the RAF were fighting back furiously. Over in Germany the fat Reichsmarschall of the Luftwaffe huffed and puffed and declared: 'This is the historic hour when our air force for the first time delivers its stroke right into the enemy's heart.' But our Spitfires and Hurricanes and our guns denied him his knock-out blow.

After nine months it seemed a useless exercise to keep on bombing a London that refused to be subdued. Finally the High Command in the Reichstag realized the wastage of manpower and materials was too high. Hitler ordered that the war effort be diverted to the USSR where the Russian bear was beginning to growl.

The raids over London slackened but the cost had been great in human suffering. Forty-eight thousand Londoners were killed or wounded during the Blitz, and thousands were made homeless. At the same time, as many innocent lives were being sacrificed in Berlin – and all on account of one bloody little megalomaniac.

Rescue workers in the remains of an Oxford Street building.

The remains of a building on Oxford Street after a night-long air raid.

Bomb-damaged shops on Oxford Steet, with a warning notice for would-be looters. There was in fact very little looting.

Buildings on Oxford Street,
shaken by explosions and
bomb-blasts, have to be
shored up with heavy
timbers.

A temporary bridge straddles a bomb crater in Charing Cross Road.

Shattered windows and a broken clock at Bourne & Hollingsworth on Oxford Street.

43

Answering a call to a bombed
house in a residential
district.   45

Rescue workers dig
frantically in the rubble in the
hope of finding survivors.

A Heavy Rescue worker at
dawn treats himself to a
hard-earned cigarette.

**A Heavy Rescue squad hook
up their trailer of equipment.**

**Early morning in London after
a night's raid.**

Weary air-raid wardens.

An elderly shopkeeper
sweeps up the broken glass
from his shattered windows.

Enemy planes are spotted
overhead as anxious passers-by
take refuge in an air-raid shelter.   53

The Revd Paul Clifford visits
an elderly couple who refused
to move out from his badly
bombed parish.

Overnight a water-filled bomb crater has replaced a parishioner's neat home.

55

Clothing donated by the public is sorted by women volunteers and distributed to casualties.

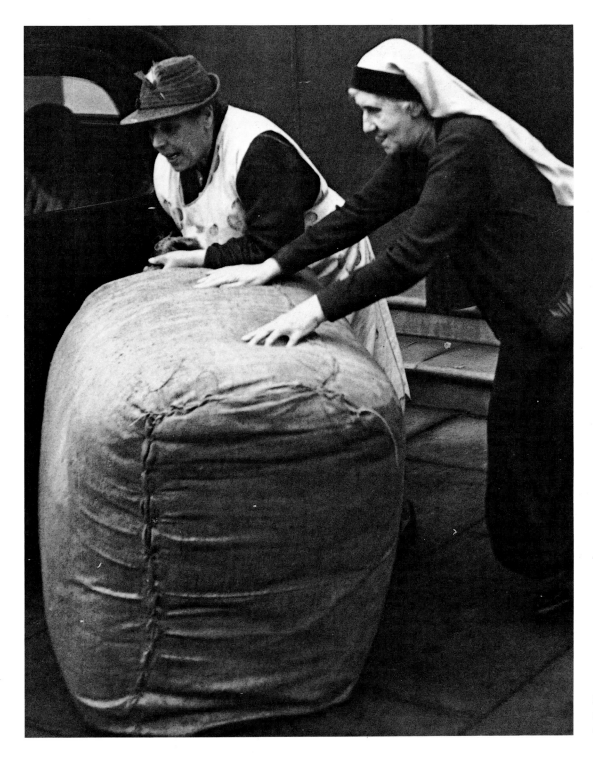

Bales of blankets are
trundled into a casualty
centre by voluntary workers. 57

**The streets of Coventry on
the morning of 15 November.**

**Smouldering ruins around
Coventry Cathedral.**

Smoke hangs in the air, but
the Union Jack still flies.

A resident salvages what he can from his blitzed home.

A bomb-dazed woman
searches the wreckage of her
home for treasured possessions. 63

A car in Coventry is buried under the wreckage of fallen buildings.

A mangled bus-stop.

Rescue workers arrive to search the rubble and to identify the dead still lying in the street.

A Coventry postman setting
out on his round finds that
many addresses have
disappeared overnight.

Food-rationing came into force in January 1940 – meat, sugar, cheese and butter at first. Tea wasn't rationed until six months later. A humanitarian Ministry of Food realized the

4 ONE LUMP OR TWO?

psychological significance of a cockney's traditional 'cuppa' and maintained an unrestricted supply for as long as possible. When, after 7 September, night-long raids became a regular affair, each shelter had a liberal supply which was presided over by the warden. Many a bomb victim was saved from shock by a steaming hot mugful with powdered milk stirred in and an extra sugar lump added surreptiously from the warden's pocket.

I was fortunate in being a coffee-drinker, for coffee was never rationed. This made my tea ration a barterable asset. Having a sweet tooth, I exchanged it with the girls in my office for their sugar ration. I developed the habit of carrying a few lumps of sugar in my camera bag. The amount of comfort these could bring, compared to so small an outlay, was beyond proportion.

The Ministry of Food granted extra tea and sugar supplies to street canteens also, and these were set up in heavily bombed areas and manned by volunteer helpers, often before the all-clear sirens had sounded. As many cups and mugs as possible were supplied by the volunteers, the rest were salvaged from wherever they could be found.

Civil-defence wardens who have been up all night are grateful for a morning cuppa.

For the lucky few, tea is still served in china cups.

A canteen is up and running at dawn for people whose homes have been damaged during the night's air raids.

Volunteer helpers arrive with food and clothing and – most importantly – tea to comfort the victims of the Blitz.

71

Two postmen take a break from their rounds for a cup of tea and a discussion of the latest air raid.

A YMCA tea car in Coventry.

5 LIFE ON THE STREETS

Once war was declared the faint-hearted gradually drifted out of London, and so, by the time the first serious daylight bombing started, the population had been thoroughly culled and the streets were emptied of all but those who were prepared to stand up to whatever Hitler had in store for us. Buses and taxis continued to operate, but, with petrol in short supply, private cars were very few and far between. Since transport was at a premium, the public crowded onto any vehicle going in the right direction. Those who did not use public transport got around by foot or bicycle. What most struck me was the unexpected speed at which we could adapt to the very rigorous conditions and the ever-present threat to our lives.

In normal times a very small number of Londoners are run over by buses or slip on banana-skins and break their legs. But suddenly in September 1940, out of a clear-blue sky, death rained down on us indiscriminately. For the first time the entire population of London was on the same level, put there by courtesy of the droning bombers of Hermann Goering's famed Luftwaffe. They came in formation, swimming like fish into the wide blue bowl of the sky with the sun reflecting from their silver sides. Just as pretty as could be. But they were fish that laid lethal eggs and we could watch the eggs falling on us to establish our common jeopardy.

Maybe Goering heard of the contempt in which we held his vaunted Luftwaffe and tried to arouse us by fitting whistles to his bombs.

But we were not impressed and, instead of calling them bombs any more, we christened them 'screaming meemies'.

The first bombs shattered the windows of the big stores. During many of these raids, there was more injury from flying glass than from the bombs themselves. Since large panes of glass were unobtainable, display windows were reduced in size and the surrounding blocked-out areas decorated by murals or, as December approached, by messages of Christmas cheer. The owners of damaged stores worked as fast as they could to repair their premises, while continuing to trade – it was a matter of pride that no shop ever remained closed unless it had been completely destroyed.

With the thought of possible invasion still uppermost in public as well as official minds, concrete tank-traps were constructed in London streets (I doubt that they would have trapped many tanks, had they been put to the test). Five-thousand-gallon water-tanks for use in fire-bomb raids were erected at strategic points all over London. In the evening the streets were virtually empty – most people tried to get home before the nightly raids began.

But the change in our daily lives was not all due to bombs. There was revolution on the home front. Rationing made each housewife view her kitchen in a new light. How far, for instance, could a single egg be made to go? And it was inconvenient when all her aluminium saucepans had been surrendered to make Spitfires. If that were not enough, she had to cook supper in the dark if the ordered black-out

A news vendor offers the
latest war news.

material had not arrived on time. There was a heavy run on light-proof black sateen. There was a restriction on water, too – voluntarily imposed – and it was no idle gesture, as every drop was needed by the fire brigade to douse nightly fires started by incendiaries.

Although the night raids after 7 September were intense and bombs were plastered all over London at random, there was still entertainment for those who dared risk it. There were theatres, concerts and cinemas, as long as they remained intact, though the curtains came down a little earlier. The Windmill Theatre remained open throughout the war. Regardless of how close bombs might fall, the show went on. I don't know if the girls in the chorus line were decorated for valour, but they should have been. It took guts to perform on stage night after night and then, when the non-stop review was over, bed down in the Windmill underground dormitory or venture alone into the noisy darkness. Maybe they weren't alone. Who cares? There was a war on and two were as vulnerable as one.

Though the Windmill was spared, many buildings in the vicinity suffered badly. Oxford Street, with its huge department stores, and Piccadilly were badly damaged. The bombs played strange tricks. They might demolish half a house but leave the rest standing. In Notting Hill Gate a man was stranded in his bath three flights above ground as the wall blew out. He waved from his tub to the firemen who erected ladders to rescue him. I, too, had a bathroom episode. I was having a drink with *Life*'s bureau chief in a house in the West End. I crossed the hall to the toilet and, as I pulled the chain – long in those days with a ceramic handle –

there was an unusually loud explosion. The house shuddered and the outside wall fell away, leaving me still holding the handle and gazing out over London.

These made good conversation-pieces on the Underground next morning where, for the first time in British history, people spoke to each other on their way to work.

Then there was Ninette – petite, just five feet two inches of radiant happiness and as pretty as a picture. She was an air-raid warden.

She was off duty that night. We danced in a Soho dungeon, and were lucky to find a taxi to take us home while the raid was still on. It was a particularly loud one and, around midnight, I phoned to make sure she was safe, as she lived alone.

There was no reply. The line was dead.

Anxiously I walked the mile to her house.

It was no longer there.

We had been dancing a few hours earlier. I could still smell the scent of her hair, and Ella Fitzgerald with the Ink Spots had sung, 'Into each life some rain must fall.'

It echoed still in my mind, and I went back to work.

Gray's Inn Road is sealed off after a night raid.

Piccadilly Circus, October 1940.

Only the buses are left running as petrol-rationing takes effect.

Shoppers find it easier to examine goods in Oxford Street stores when windows have been blasted out.

Nylons are beginning to get scarce.

Londoners go about their business on a quieter than usual Oxford Street.

Oxford Circus after the first bomb fell in August 1940.

The Paddington station-
master selects some records
to hearten commuters.

An Oxford Street news
vendor.

The forces information office,
Trafalgar Square.

A soldier on leave.

People gather below Nelson's Column for a lunch-time concert.

89

Red Cross flag day on
Tottenham Court Road.

Rapid repair work is carried out on a shop front.

A topical mural decorates a bomb-blasted shop front.

A group of elderly East End residents are evacuated.

This news vendor flatly
refused to take shelter during
raids.

Downing Street, guarded by a sandbagged machine-gun nest.

Tank-traps in a London street.

Emergency water-tanks also serve as poster hoardings.

Passers-by anxiously scan the night's casualty list ...

... praying not to find the
name of a friend or relative.

A householder manages to salvage a family picture.

The streets emptied after dark. People went home as long as transport was available but a few happy revellers did the rounds of the underground night spots. The Hungaria in Soho

6 LIFE UNDERGROUND

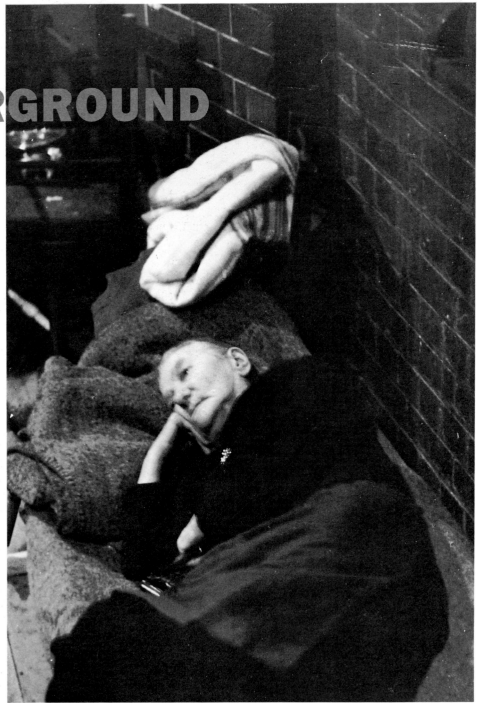

was our favourite haunt. In 1940 there was still a good supply of vintage wines and brandy. There was good food and a live Hungarian band for dancing, all in what was once the cellar of the restaurant. If, during dinner, the raids became too close for comfort, the proprietor bedded down his guests on camp-beds and served them breakfast next morning, wearing his blue silk dressing-gown.

Bars and cafés and office-parties all went underground. The sorting offices of the GPO were below ground, most of Whitehall too – Churchill referred to his office staff as 'fellow troglodytes'. Girls working in the various Ministries had their underground canteens and dormitories, and below the Ministry of Defence there was an underground chapel.

Many of the charitable associations arranged shelters in disused factory cellars, and, of course, the safest place of a night was the London Underground. As darkness fell, thousands drifted down to claim a few yards of cold, bare platform. Before long, particular spots were recognized as belonging to particular people. A white line, three feet from the edge of the platform assured access to the trains for would-be passengers. Everyone felt secure down there until, one night, not far from Marble Arch, a bomb penetrated through to the platform and killed 300 people. Nowhere, it seemed, was really safe.

An elderly Londoner sleeps
rough.

A community air-raid shelter
in the East End.

An underground canteen
provides early-morning tea for
air-raid victims.

One of London's many cellar bars.

An office shelter during a daytime raid.

The women's services'
personnel in Whitehall had
their own underground
canteen ...

... and a small chapel built beneath the Ministry of Defence.

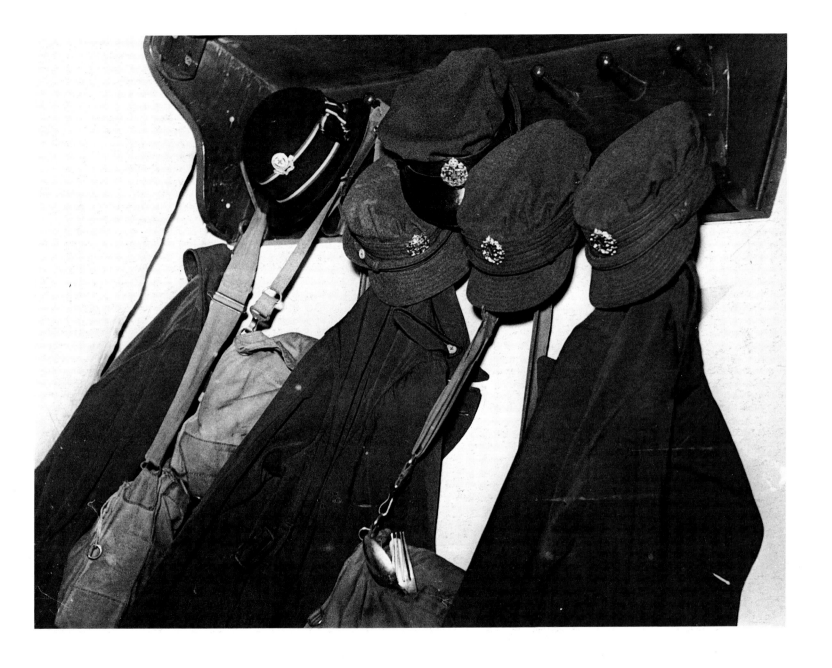

A coat-rack displays the hats
of the WRNS, WAAF and ATS.   111

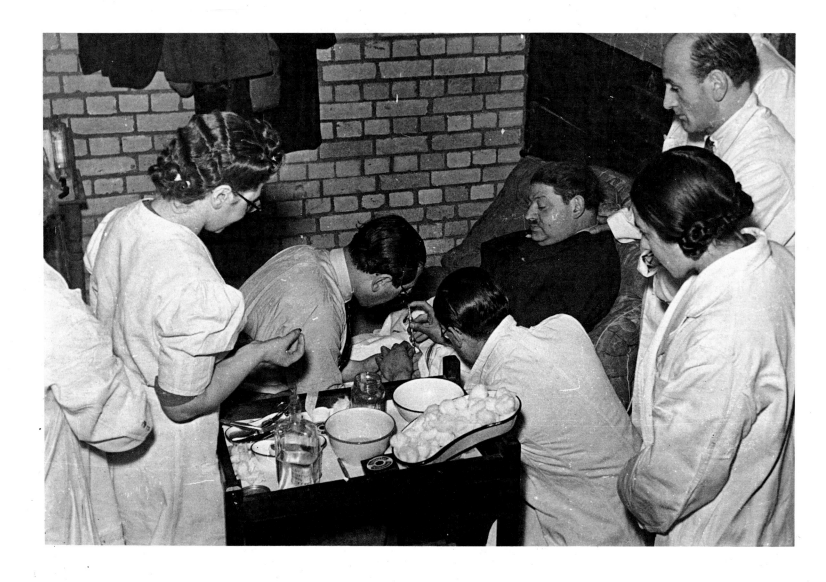

A first-aid room in an underground shelter – the majority of minor injuries were caused by flying glass.

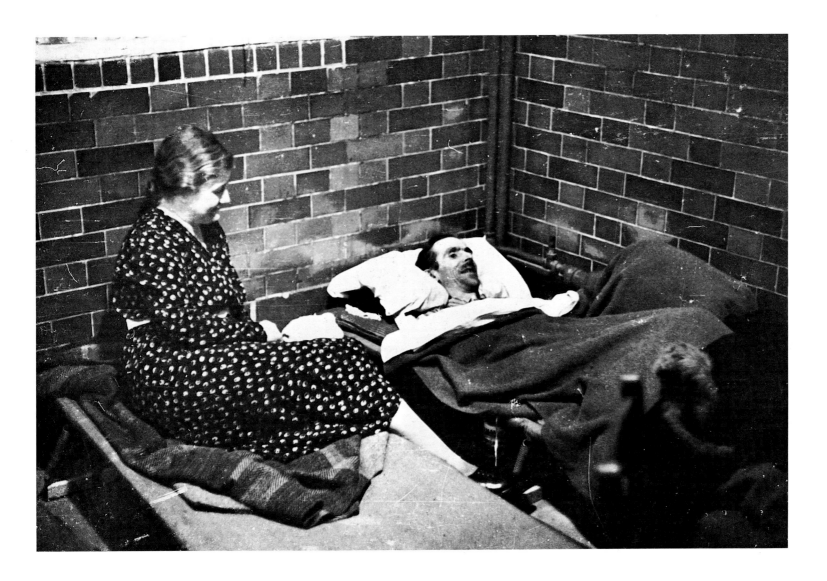

A woman watches over her
injured husband.

The proprietor of the Hungaria ...

... where brandy and cigars
could still be enjoyed ...

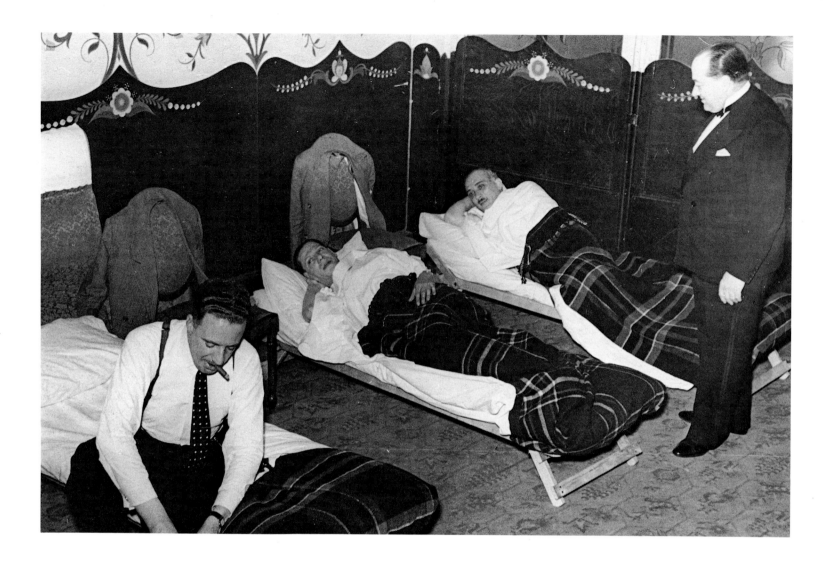

... as well as a bed for the night ...

... and breakfast in the morning.

Hymn-singing in a community shelter.

Everybody tucked in for the
night.

7 THE CHILDREN'S BLITZ

As the threat of war became imminent, the government initiated a massive evacuation programme. Over two million people had to be moved from the vulnerable parts of Britain to places of greater safety. About a million of these were children.

It must be remembered that, immediately after the declaration of war, every kind of Nazi horror was expected and the widely publicized fate of Poland, Holland, Belgium and France was in everybody's mind. Quietly but rapidly the children were taken from the danger zones and, before the year 1939 was out, five out of every six of London's children had left the city. They had been hustled out by train, with a toothbrush and a gas- mask and very little else, to destinations that were unknown to them. Very few mothers were able to accompany their offspring.

This, of course, was a Government-sponsored programme and foster homes were ready to receive them. Better-off families were able to make their own arrangements to send their children out of the country altogether. They went mostly to America, Canada, South Africa and some to Australia. This led to the tragedy of the Ellerman liner *City of Benares* which was torpedoed 600 miles into the Atlantic. Of the 260 people who lost their lives, 79 were children on their way to Canada.

By Christmas 1939 nothing particularly drastic had happened to London. Children began to filter back to their families and, for these, the London shops stocked toys with a military theme: clockwork tanks and troop-carriers; model Spitfires and bombers; guns of all kinds and lead soldiers. For the girls there were dolls, but they were in uniform: ATS, WRNS and WAAFS, as true to life as possible. Some were even holding cigarettes.

A few children were unlucky enough to be in hospital during the 1940 raids. But, as in the case of Great Ormond Street Hospital, there were shelters deep underground provided with wooden bunks. Nurses rushed them down as soon as the sirens sounded.

Those children who were up and about on the London streets did not spend their days idly, although all schools in the Greater London area had been evacuated to the country. There were plenty of jobs to be done, and many youngsters were mobilized by Aneurin Bevan for tasks such as metal-collection. There was no such thing as an ordinary day for the children of the Blitz.

A young East-Ender wears his
helmet with pride.

An ARP warden chalks up an evacuation rota.

Parents and children crowd Paddington Station.

A mother and daughter wait forlornly at Paddington Station.

Some children are returned to school ...

... while others depart for
unknown destinations.

A community-shelter
canteen.

Bedtime prayers during a raid ...

... and the children stay wide
awake as the bombs fall.

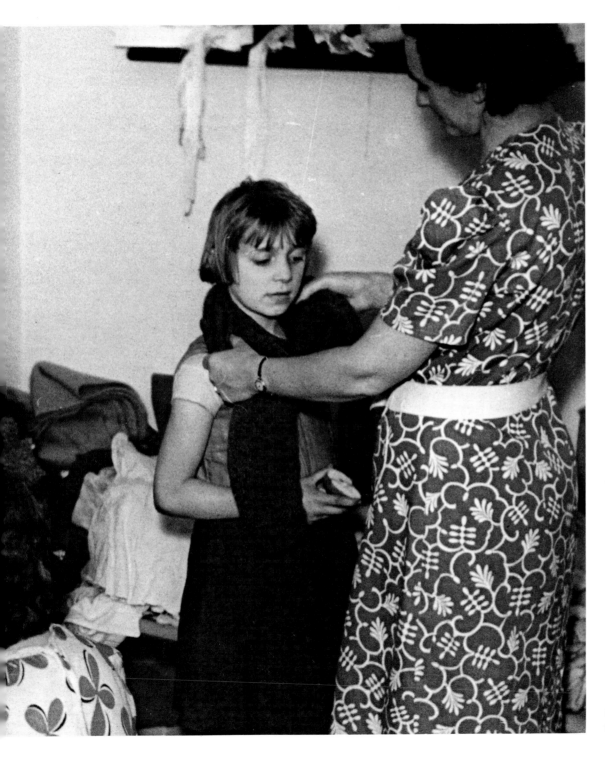

**Children in a casualty station
are given fresh clothing.** 131

Coventry. The morning after
the 'Baedecker' raid:
a mother and her children ...

...and a family who have lost
their house during the night.

Children crane their necks to watch an aerial dog-fight over the Grand Hotel, Dover, studiously ignored by the older generation.

Dover. A woman shelters from shrapnel.

Schoolboys admire the model planes in an Oxford Street toy-shop.

Rank upon rank of lead soldiers fill John Lewis's Christmas shop-window.

These Coventry boys have just been dug out of the rubble of their homes.

It dawned on the British public very fast that if commodities they were used to were no longer available, they might as well do without and be cheerful about it.

8 BUSINESS AS USUAL

Shopkeepers, too, were determined to serve their customers as though nothing had happened, even if their shop fronts had been blown out in the night. Shops always opened unless they had been completely destroyed, even if customers had to pick their way through rubble to make their purchases. Popular among bargain-hunters were the salvage sales at which goods damaged during air raids, when shops and warehouses were destroyed, were sold at knock-down prices.

'Business as usual' became the maxim of the moment.

Sales-girls at John Lewis on Oxford Street served lingerie to customers from an improvised counter on the pavement, with the wreckage of the store behind them.

Flower-sellers picked their way through fallen rubble with laden, scented barrows.

Identity discs were on sale in shattered doorways.

During air raids, news vendors refused to leave their stands on the open streets. One lady outside Selfridge's sat quietly knitting on the pavement by her display of *Picture Post, Illustrated* and the latest war news in the dailies, although the siren had sounded and bombs were actually falling. I photographed her and bought a newspaper. She gave me my change. Nothing was said and she continued with her knitting.

In south London a woman known as Mrs Boss emerged as the champion collector of scrap metal. She bullied members of the borough into donating everything from the railings round their houses to bath-tubs and frying-pans, to be melted down and recast into munitions.

Every morning pavements were littered with glass from windows broken by blast during the night. Large shop fronts were particularly vulnerable, and staff were kept busy sweeping up the splinters.

It was hardly worth the trouble of replacing broken windows only to have them blown out again, and, anyway, glass was soon in short supply. Shop fronts were boarded up and decorated with cartoons or snappy 'business as usual' slogans – quite discreet in the West End, but a little bawdier in the East, directed personally at Hitler.

People disliked having the routine of their lives upset, but it does seem paradoxical, with all the rubble in the streets, to find a charlady on hands and knees scrubbing the floor in a shop entrance, or a man with a Marylebone Borough Council dust-cart sweeping the pavement.

Perhaps it was the inability of Hitler and his high command to recognize the resolution of the British people that finally helped lose them the war.

A message of defiance to the
Führer.

Housewives queue for eggs.

The milkman was a familiar
and reliable sight.

Barrow boys at Marble Arch.

One of the last barrows of bananas.

Shop-steps are still scrubbed each morning.

A salvage sale in a men's outfitters: before ...

... and after.

**Bomb-damaged goods are
offered at bargain prices.**

**John Lewis on Oxford Street
was badly damaged ...**

... but in no time the
assistants set up shop on the
pavement.

Fleet Street.

W. H. Smith's at Paddington
Station.

As bomb-blast shatters glass, some businesses dispense with shop fronts altogether.

An organ-grinder on Oxford Street.

A cellar bar does a brisk trade.

The underground sorting
offices of the GPO.

**Mrs Boss, the champion
scrap-metal collector, at work
in the streets ...**

... and in her East End depot.

Although to be vindictive is not a British characteristic, a stubborn determination to stand up for our rights is. In doing so, the RAF did to Berlin what the Luftwaffe did to London,

9 HIT BACK!

and the result proved the ghastly wastage and folly of a war that nobody wanted to fight – nobody that is but a handful of the top brass in the German Reichstag.

Not a single head of state throughout the world gave Britain a dog's chance of standing up to Hitler's 'Total Annihilation'. But in our sceptered isle nobody from Winston Churchill down gave defeat a thought. What was broken down by Goering's bombers we built up again, often with bare hands.

'Business as usual Mr Hitler' was chalked on the ruins of a small shop which represented a man's life savings. On the hoarding that covered the front of a larger store were the words 'Shattered but not Shuttered.' And again, a furniture store, with no glass left in its windows but a sense of humour surviving in the proprietor, announced: 'They can smash our windows but they can't beat our furnishing values!' Everywhere was the slogan 'Hit Back!' 'Hit Back!'

We hit back, and, after the Luneberg Surrender, five years later, on my way to Denmark, I had the personal satisfaction of driving my jeep, with the Union Jack flying, through the remnants of the defeated German Army in Schleswig-Holstein. There were soldiers in their thousands. I was alone and, though they were unaware the war was over, they were too demoralized even to notice me.

Propaganda posters urge the
public to caution.

A news vendor displays a
variety of wartime reading. 161

A snack bar offers a special
'air raid breakfast'.

Oxford Circus.

A sandwich-man on Oxford
Street.

A sale aims to attract
patriotic bargain-hunters.

Even having a haircut became risky business.

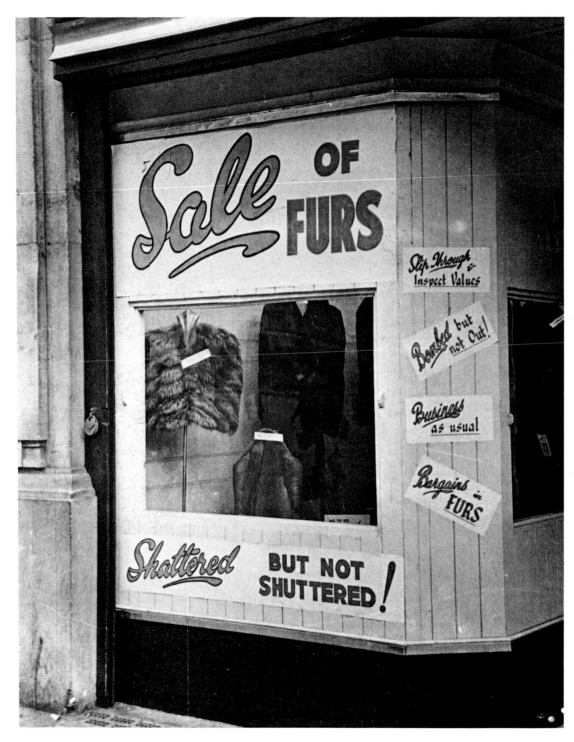

Bargain prices beat the
bombs ...

... and Christmas greetings
challenge the Führer.   171

**The British sense of humour
still prevails.**

Passers-by are exhorted to make donations to the Spitfire fund.

A street vendor does a brisk
trade in identity discs.

Shops display patriotic messages.

A prescient effigy of Hitler hangs from a shattered bus-stop in Whitehall.